AWAKENING NEW LIFE

AWAKENING NEW LIFE

21 Day Journey to Freedom

JESSICA NANCE

I want to dedicate this book to an amazing group of christian prayer warriors from North Carolina that have supported the movement of the Holy Spirit. A special thank you to Ginger Klausing and Ann Reed for your support in making this book possible for the body of Christ.

INTRODUCTION

HOW TO USE THE WORKBOOK

START

    DAY 1-- SAYING NO

    DAY 2-- WHO ARE THE JONESES ANYWAY?

    DAY 3-- WHAT IS IMPORTANT?

EXPAND

    DAY 4-- SURRENDER= FREEDOM

    DAY 5-- ASK HIM TO CLEAN HOUSE

    DAY 6-- DON'T FORGET YOUR EARS!

EXPLODE

    DAY 7-- LESS PRESSURE

    DAY 8-- IF IT DOESN'T FLOW, YOU DON'T GO

    DAY 9-- ANXIETY AND JESUS CANNOT COEXIST

EXPLORE

    DAY 10-- HOW DID GOD DO IT?

    DAY 11-- NARROW YOUR FOCUS

    DAY 12-- REAL REST

SOAK IN IT

    DAY 13-- ADVENTURE AWAITS!

    DAY 14-- LIVE FEARLESSLY

    DAY 15-- SEEK 1ST THE KINGDOM

SEEK

    DAY 16-- WHO DOES GOD SAY YOU ARE?

    DAY 17-- WHAT IS YOUR SPIRITUAL GIFT?

    DAY 18-- HOW TO SUCCEED

SALE

    DAY 19-- EVERYTHING OUT OF LOVE

    DAY 20-- WHAT DO YOU HAVE TO GIVE?

    DAY 21-- GIVE GOD THE PRAISE

INTRODUCTION

What purpose does God have for my life? How can the Holy Spirit use me when I do not even have time for family? Am I getting it right or wrong in life?

This is a 21-day journey into experiencing real freedom and relying fully on God the Father, Son, and Holy Spirit. This workbook and program was written by the Holy Spirit and will have a different outcome for each participant. He desires for the church to come back to him! Let us lay down our traditions, denominational walls and our personal thoughts to hear what God has to say.

Jesus paid the ultimate sacrifice so that we can live in freedom! Christians are sometimes the worst at allowing the enemy to keep us in chains and bondage. We call it weird, improper, or say, "That's not the way we have always done it" when God says to live freely through the Holy Spirit.

This workbook is going to be different in each individual's walk with the Lord, but we suggest finding a great group of Christians to experience the journey together so you can share thoughts, prayer, and hold each other accountable in the process. It is full of hard questions that could challenge your current walk. It will help you invite the Holy Spirit to change your heart and prepare you for revival!

Let us WAKE UP CHURCH! Let us not be asleep when Christ returns. I pray this sparks the flame for every Christian heart so we can become disciples and go and make disciples!

This is a seven-part workbook containing three days per each section. Each section also contains a video to help guide you through the journey. Each day contains a topic, challenge, three questions and scripture for meditation.

1. Before starting each day, invite the Holy Spirit into your heart to help you see, hear, and feel what He has for you that day
2. Read through the topic slowly and repeat as needed to get a full understanding of what God is saying
3. Answer and act on the challenge given
4. Answer the questions
5. Meditate on the scripture provided

It is ok to take more than 21 days on this journey to freedom if you feel led to take more time on particular topics. We encourage finding ways to express your thoughts to the Lord outside of this workbook. Some will use music to help them get into a spirit of worship, some will journal prayers and others may use the blank spaces to display art.

No matter what the journey holds, know that you are not alone! Reach out to our team for support or prayer at AwakeningNewLife.com

1 Corinthians 2:9 "What no eye has seen, what no ear has heard, and what no human mind has conceived'-- the things God has prepared for those who love him"

STEP ONE- START

DAY 1-- STOP OVERLOADING!

Why do we overload ourselves, allowing in a seed of stress that leads straight to anxiety? That little seed of saying, "Yes" all the time is what the enemy wants. He wants to create as many items on our calendar as possible, so we don't have "time" for reading our Bible, singing praises to Jesus or even showing your family God's love. The enemy doesn't even have to try that hard to get you to do "good" things, like cutting construction paper and gluing eyes on a juice box to make kids smile or adding a volunteer opportunity to your already booked calendar. He is using the "good" things to slowly enter you into where the "good" becomes sin.

Have you considered what it would be like to say, "No?"

Have you thought or even dreamed about what it would look like to have free unplanned time blocked off in your calendar? Like the kind of time where you can play with your kids or have a cell phone free dinner with your spouse, make eye contact and talk about your passions? Do you even remember what your passions are and where they got lost in the mix of what we call adult life? Do you know that you have the power to say no to everyone else but say, "I am listening," to God?

We have created no room for God in our busy chaotic lifestyles and wonder why we feel exhausted, stressed, lonely in a crowded room. God is our provider, sustainer, and lifter of our head. How do we expect to go through life without His nourishment? We can become so distracted that we don't even know who we are or what our real purpose in this life.

Psalm 3:3 "But you, Lord, are a shield around me, my glory, the One who lifts my head high."

Challenge: Say No to the next several requests. If this puts your mind into a spiral of anxiety, simply claim victory over fear, stress, and anxiety in Jesus Name! Clear your calendar for the next 21 days and PIN DOWN. Do not add anything to your calendar no matter how good it is. Simply explain to anyone that is confused by your sudden change that you feel led to spend more time with your family and in this season, you cannot take on any other task. Now enter a season of healing and reprograming from what the world says now to what God says.

Romans 12:2 "Do not conform to the patter of this world, but be transformed by the renewing of your mind. Then you will be able to test and approve what God's will is-- his good, pleasing and perfect will."

What are my absolute requirements to do for the next 21 days? (This should only include the extreme basics of survival like work and feeding your family)

What items can I rearrange or delegate to someone else for this time during the journey

What do I need to take away from in my home life? (Example: only 1 hour of screen time for the full family...yes that means ending your 3-hour binge on Pinterest)

Verses for Meditation
Philippians 4:11-13

Who are the Jones family anyway? When did we allow an electronic device to dictate our standards to live by? What has social media really done to our lives? Is it dictating how we should try to live? How much debt do we have because we need to take the most unrealistic portrait of perfection? When did it start mattering what we eat, wear, or do?

Matthew 6:25 "Therefore I tell you, do not worry about your life, what you will eat or drink; or about your body, what you will wear. Is not life more than food, and the body more than clothes?"

God did not intend for humans to direct our path. Humans are of the world; we will fail each other. We do not have all the answers and cannot determine our eternal life. Why do we lean so heavily on what others think or say and not on what God thinks and says who we are and how we should live?

Romans 12:2 "Do not conform to the pattern of this world, but be transformed by the renewing of your mind. Then you will be able to test and approve what God's will is-- his good, pleasing, and perfect will."

The minute you sit your pride at the feet of Jesus, the quicker you will start following the good, pleasing, and perfect will of God. Our number one question is always "I do not know what God wants me to do in life?" or "I just want to be in the perfect will of God, but I like all my stuff." If we really want to know the perfect path for us, we must be willing to lay it all down. Then, allow Him to show us, daily, not just one feel good time at a moving Sunday morning service.

Hebrews 13:20-21 "Now may the God of peace, who through the blood of the eternal covenant brought back from the dead our Lord Jesus, that great Shepherd of the sheep, equip you with everything good for doing his will and may he work in us what is pleasing to him, through Jesus Christ, to whom be glory for ever and ever. Amen."

Do you remember when you were a kid, and your biggest concern was playing outside with your friends or getting silly excited that you were getting mac-n-cheese for dinner that night? Remember how simple that life was without the 'worries of the world?' Is God not our Father and we, His children? Should we not live as children to Him? Being content in all ways and get excited for little things.

Matthew 18:2-4 "He called a little child to him and placed the child among them. And he said: "Truly I tell you, unless you change and become like little children, you will never enter the kingdom of heaven. Therefore, whoever takes the lowly position of this child is the greatest in the kingdom of heaven."

Challenge: Now that you have cleared your calendar... let's look at where you are placing your value. Are you working so hard to have more "stuff" or are you working hard to build up eternal rewards? Pray about what God can remove in your heart that is blocking you from full freedom.

List three things that you have placed too much value in that you can give away today.

What distracts me from time with God? (This could take extra paper. Its ok, be honest)

What can I do with this extra free time?

Verses for Meditation
Psalm 90:12

DAY 3-- WHAT IS IMPORTANT?

We listen to motivational podcasts, read books on self-development and chat with people about how to get a better set of abs, but how much time do we spend with the One that can fix it all? When we look at our lives or are asked to list out our priorities, what do we say? Most people will throw their family on top (even if they give the kids less time than social media). Next, we add our career that we have spent most of our life trying to enhance. Then we may list a non-profit or church we love so we can round our list out to make us feel good. But in all honestly, what does our true list look like?

Most may look like this:

1. Work-- or work-related activities
2. Screen Time to disconnect from work (including social media, tv, gaming etc.)
3. House Chores (The upkeep of all the stuff we have)
4. Family (we eat together and yell at each other, out of love of course)
5. Church or God (If we have some time left over and remember to hit up those nighttime prayers with the kids)

Is this really a satisfying lifestyle? Does this make us joyful to wake up each day or do we dread the morning time routine? Can we say that we feel like we are rocking out this life by this list in order or priority?

What if we flipped this list like Jesus flipped tables? What if it looked more like this?

1. Time with Jesus
2. Family (real undistracted screen-free time)
3. Home (Taking care of what the Lord has given)
4. Disconnection time (it's really ok to disconnect our brains, but maybe consider using another means to disconnect like getting outside in nature. And really, we do love seeing the cute picture of your kiddo laughing with cake all over their faces!)
5. Work (yes, we must work to eat, and we should treat this as a mission field anyway)

Imagine that life! Imagine a world where you could just refocus your existence into glorifying your creator! No worries, no fear; just basking in His Glory. What peace we would have in our daily lives. Yes, we are not promised to live without struggles of the world but in whatever we do, we do it for the Glory of God.

1 Corinthians 10:31 "So whether you eat or drink or whatever you do, do it all for the glory of God."

Challenge: Write out your priority list (honestly). Now write the list the way you feel God would want it to be.

What are you still holding on to in your schedule? Why? (This is not to justify but expose what is still holding you back.)

What sin gets in your way from putting the King of Kings and Lord of Lords first?

How do we change it? Ask God to help you because you may need to do a full table flip! You are not alone in this process. Reach out to Godly people for help.

Verses for Meditation
1 Corinthians 10: 23-24

DAY 4-- SURRENDER= FREEDOM

Seriously? I have given up my whole calendar and have flipped the table so much my kids are now wanting me to get a hobby away from them and it's only been a few days! Now you are telling me I need to surrender more. What is left?

Romans 12:1 "Therefore, I urge you, brothers and sisters, in view of God's mercy, to offer your bodies as a living sacrifice, holy and pleasing to God--this is your true and proper worship."

So, you want me to do a weird human sacrifice now? Is this going too far? What in the world is meant by "...giving my body as a sacrifice?"

1 Corinthians 6:19-20 "Do you not know that your bodies are temples of the Holy Spirit, who is in you, whom you have received from God? You are not your own; you were bought at a price. Therefore, honor God with your bodies."

Sin ruins the temple God created. What sin are you holding on to that is blocking you from blessings? What is blocking the Holy Spirit from dwelling in you? What past deep thing is causing you to hate your temple? Did you know that God knew you before you were formed in your mother's womb and that he has a plan for you? Did you know that God loves you so much that he already paid for your yucky sin? Remember the cross? Remember what he did for you so you can live free from sin?

Jeremiah 1:5 "Before I formed you in the womb I knew you, before you were born I set you apart; I appointed you as a prophet to the nations."

But when we just keep sinning over and over again and justify it as "just being human;" did you know that we are nailing Jesus back to the cross over and over again?

Hebrews 6:4-6 "It is impossible for those who have once been enlightened, who have tasted the heavenly gift, who have shared in the Holy Spirit, who have tasted the goodness of the word of God and the powers of the coming age and who have fallen away, to be brought back to repentance. To their loss they are crucifying the Son of God all over again and subjecting him to public disgrace."

Challenge: Ask God to fill you with the Holy Spirit so you can taste and know the goodness of God! You may have asked to be saved, but have you FULLY SURRENDERED?

What sin is holding me back from the full goodness of God? (Not what you need to work on, but what you need to ask Jesus to get rid of.)

How do I know the Holy Spirit is there? Ask God to first clean out your heart fully so you can surrender your life and ask Him to fill your heart back up with the Holy Spirit. How do you feel now?

What do I feel Him leading me to do now?

Verses for Meditation
Hebrews 2: 14-18

For some of you this may mean physically and to all it means internally. When we look around our actual house, what do we see that is important vs what we can live without? When we look internally at our heart, what do we see that is important vs what we can live without? God wants it all. Are we willing to give up our worldly possessions and follow God's lead when he says go? Are we willing to give up a grudge we have kept toward a family member that destroyed relationships? Or what about the sin of overindulgence in food or lust of the body? It may seem harmless in the moment, but it gets rooted in our heart and grows!

Matthew 16: 24-25 "Then Jesus said to his disciples, Whoever wants to be my disciple must deny themselves and take up their cross and follow me. For whoever wants to save his life will lose it, but whoever loses his life for me will find it."

When you read this verse, you may think geez, what kind of cruel God asks me to die for Him or give up my great life? "I have worked hard for all my stuff, right?" God is not having you evaluate if he loves you enough, it is if you love HIM enough. We KNOW God loves you because he sent his only Son to become partly human to feel and know sin the way we do and die for US so we can live eternally! The question is: Are you willing to do the same? Would you be willing to follow Jesus straight to the cross?

This is deep and for some, hard to process this in our hearts and minds. When we proclaim, "What would Jesus do?" Do we really think about that or just wear it on a bracelet?

Challenge: Take time to clean out your home and heart. Ask God what you have that you do not need that may bless someone else? While you are putting items in bags to donate, ask God to reveal what you still have left deep down in your heart that needs to be cleaned out. This process may hurt in the moment but trust the journey!

What makes you react in anger when something or someone is brought up in conversation?

What hurt or lies have you been told (even from as far back as childhood) that still bring pain?

Ask Jesus, "What now?" He can clean up even our biggest messes!

Verses for Meditation
Psalm 139: 1-6

We are so good at talking, but how good are we at listening? We tend to struggle with this in the natural and wonder why we can't hear God in the supernatural? How do we hear God's voice? How does he speak?

Psalm 119:105 "Your word is a lamp for my feet, a light on my path."

God speaks to us in many ways!

1. The Word of God (Bible): *2 Timothy 3:16 "All Scripture is God-breathed and is useful for teaching, rebuking, correcting, and training in righteousness."*
2. Prophetically (Direct Words): *Jeremiah 1:9 "Then the Lord reached out his hand and touched my mouth and said to me, 'I have put my words in your mouth."*
3. Through the Holy Spirit (From Others, Dreams, Visions): *Joel 2:28 "And it shall come to pass afterward, that I will pour out my Spirit on all flesh; your sons and your daughters shall prophesy, your old men shall dream dreams, and your young men shall see visions".*
4. Messengers (Angels): *Revelation 19:9 "Then the angel said to me, 'Write this: Blessed are those who are invited to the wedding supper of the Lamb!' And he added, 'These are the true words of God.'"*
5. Nature: *Psalm 19:1 "The heavens declare the glory of God; the skies proclaim the work of his hands."*

God wants you to be so close to him that you know his voice even in the small things or in the whispers.

Matthew 10: 27 "What I tell you in the dark, speak in the daylight; what is whispered in your ear, proclaim from the roofs."

With this, it is worth warning that the other side likes to try to deceive you in whispers too! So, make sure that you discern the spirits and know the voice of the Father by confirming what you are hearing using scripture.

1 John 4:1 "Dear friends, do not believe every spirit, but test the spirits to see whether they are from God, because many false prophets have gone out into the world."

Challenge: Ask God to help you know His voice. Create scheduled time every day to get into His Word so you can get to know Him more! It's okay to mark this in the calendar and it's okay to include your kids and spouse. He has placed you together for this time to grow together!

Have you heard a word or song that, "oddly" came on at that perfect time? What did it say? Could that have been a whisper from God?

Has God talked to you clearly before? If not, ask God to speak to you and listen for it!

If you were face to face with Jesus, what would you want him to say?

Verses for Meditation
Colossians 1:9-14

STEP 3- EXPLODE

DAY 7-- LESS PRESSURE

Jesus did not go to the cross for us to bare the burden of our sin and shortfalls. Of course, we live in a world where the enemy can make it hard to take the right path, but we are the ones with the authority of Jesus Christ to walk boldly. This life really should not be "hard" because we have the power of angel armies behind us as long as we are submitted to Jesus! Knowing the sheer power you have in you through the Holy Spirit creates much less pressure on your human nature. The words you speak and the actions you take when lead by the Spirit should be effortless.

Jeremiah 1:9 "Then the Lord reached out his hand and touched my mouth and said to me, 'I have put my words in your mouth.'"

We do not have to live worried about what we will say or do for the Lord. All we must do is seek Him FIRST and worship Him. Then he will place the words or song in our mouths to proclaim.

Matthew 6:33 "But seek first his kingdom and his righteousness, and all these things will be given to you as well."

Thank you, Jesus, for taking life's pressures off our shoulders. Thank you, Lord, for caring about us enough to bare the cross and erase the mess away!

Anxiety and Jesus cannot exist in the same space. If you are still feeling overwhelmed, nervous, or anxious about anything or even about walking fully surrendered to the King of Kings; just start praising God. Worship and worry cannot exist in the same space. Let the praise of your mouth be your weapon in this battle to claim victory and freedom over your life!

Philippians 4:6-7 "Do not be anxious about anything, but in every situation, by prayer and petition, with thanksgiving, present your request to God. And the peace of God, which transcends all understanding, will guard your hearts and your minds in Christ Jesus."

Challenge: Evaluate your reactions. What makes you react quickly out of anger or will get you nervous easily? Write them down. Now, take a red pen and strike them out!! Jesus's blood paid for that already! Give it over to him and breathe out thankfulness.

What is weighing on your shoulders? Is it in or out of your control to change it?

What scares you about walking into full surrender to Jesus?

How do you fight your battles?

Verse for Meditation
Ephesians 6:12-13

Have you ever had a day were nothing goes right? Or, maybe for years it has seemed like you've been on the losing end constantly? Have you said to yourself or to God, "I just don't know what I am doing wrong to always be on the struggle bus?" Sometimes we just think the enemy uses us as a punching bag or that mankind has it out for us.

Have we thought about nothing going right because we are on the wrong path? Maybe we opened a door that should have been shut? Or slammed a door that should have been opened? Have we asked about the door to the creator of the door?

Matthew 7:7-8 "Ask and it will be given to you; seek and you will find; knock and the door will be opened to you. For everyone who asks receives; the one who seeks finds; and to the one who knocks, the door will be opened."

If you rolled your eyes, stop a minute. Maybe you have asked for direction and feel that God didn't answer your prayer. Let us take time to think about that moment. What did we ask for? Why do you think God didn't answer or give you the desired outcome? What if He did answer, but you had too much sin coming into your ears that was blocking what His whisper was saying? Or if He would have answered what you thought was right, it could have caused something more major to go wrong over time. Possibly it was not time for such event or change to take place.

We do not see the big picture of our life but our Creator does. We place so much value on our human minds describing how life should look based on what the world says. If we are truly seeking first his Kingdom, then what the world says around us drowns out and we can ask, seek and know why something went differently than we prayed.

Challenge: Think of a time something did not go the way you planned and ask God why. If you saw the outcome was really Him protecting you, thank Him. Either way, God sees it all and gets all the glory and praise (even when we don't see)!

What do you think it looks like on a deeper level to ask, seek, and knock?

What sin or rooted issue is still hidden in your heart? Are you holding on to what is blocking you from answers and full communication with God?

Ask God if you are in His perfect will for your life. Is there anything you are doing that you know is outside of His will for you?

Verses for Meditation
Matthew 7: 13-14

One of the number one problems Christians struggle with today is anxiety. We allow anxiety that the enemy first places in our minds to sink into our whole bodies until we start believing and claiming the lie. Jesus and anxiety are not allowed in the same room. Many Christians have said, "I struggle with anxiety or depression and just can't get on the stage to sing." Or "I'm too nervous to speak up when someone is speaking lies to my friend, what would they say about me?"

God knows us inside and out. There may very well be an underlying medical imbalance that is contributing to these feelings. Ask which ask the creator of your body to reveal that to you. But otherwise, it is a sheer attack from the enemy. If the other side can get you to stop doing the perfect will of God or oppresses you, he gains a victory. Do NOT allow this!

How do we battle it? We must pray to bind up the enemy and release the good! If the slight thought of "I am not good enough" or "I can't, because I struggle too much on the inside" comes along, BIND IT UP IN JESUS NAME and say YES, I CAN IN JESUS NAME! It is time for the Church to start gaining back ground we have lost from the enemy and taking back the gifts God has blessed us with abundantly!

> *Matthew 16:19 "I will give you the keys of the kingdom of heaven; whatever you bind on earth will be bound in heaven, and whatever you loose on earth will be loosed in heaven."*

Challenge: Do it! Jesus has given you all authority to bind up the evil one in any situation and release the good in it! Speak LIFE NOT DEATH even when it seems hopeless!

What do you speak over yourself? Do you look in the mirror and speak beauty or flaws? Do you claim joy over sorrow?

What do you speak over your spouse or children? Do you speak full encouragement, or do you talk down to them? Do you have them believing the lie or the truth?

What evil is lingering that you can cast out in Jesus Name?

Verses for Meditation
1 Peter 3:8-9

DAY 10-- HOW DID GOD DO IT?

When we go back to the creation of the world and of mankind, what comes to mind? Was it the fact that God formed all the amazing details or that he just spoke, and things formed? There is so much we can gain in knowledge just by looking at the first page of the Bible. The fact that he took 7 days to make everything good, why? Couldn't he just blink and all of it be done at the same time?

Do you think there is a lesson in this and how we are to live? We have an amazing example of how to live through the accounts of Jesus's life, but do we take it back to creation and the beauty in the journey. The beauty in the process of forming something so amazing that mankind has not even discovered all the different animals of the sea.

Why do we rush our lives? Why do we feel like we have to have every detail perfectly designed in a day? Even the CREATOR of the WORLD had a process and claimed that it was good. Then on top of that, he took a day to rest. Do you really think God needed a resting day? Or, was it for us to see and understand how we are designed and what we need in our own bodies?

Genesis 2:1-3 "Thus the heavens and the earth were completed in all their vast array. By the seventh day God had finished the work he had been doing; so, on the seventh day he rested from all his work. Then God blessed the seventh day and made it holy, because on it he rested from all the work of creating that he had done."

Are we finding rest? Are we keeping our seventh day holy and just for Him? God wants us to look deeper at how he works. He has given us the Bible to look at the examples of His nature and the nature of the Trinity (Father, Son and Holy Spirit).

Challenge: We have already started clearing our calendars, but now Ask God what you need to do on His holy day? What should you stop doing?

What does rest look like? Why do you think it was important to God during creation?

How can we be like God? How can we do good work and then find peaceful rest?

What would your family benefit from if you laid down your phones, TV and social media to find rest with them? How would your family change if you were resting together?

Verses for Meditation
Genesis 1:1-31

Now that we have cleaned house, cleaned up our heart, taken back what is ours and rested; what now? Now, we can fix our eyes on what God wants for our life. If we are truly seeking first His Kingdom, then he is going to add things to us. This path may seem narrow, and few will go through it; but what is on the other side is worth the squeezing that is taking place!

Matthew 7:14 "But small is the gate and narrow the road that leads to life, and only a few find it."

Tight spaces may frighten some of you, but what this small space leads to is worth the narrow path. Will some think you are weird at this point? Probably. Will some say you are crazy and just taking this Jesus thing a little too far? Absolutely. Do you care? Nope.

Matthew 10:22 "You will be hated by everyone because of me, but the one who stands firm to the end will be saved."

Challenge: Write down what you would be willing to give up for Jesus? If He called you by name to go and do something for Him, what would you be willing to do, or not willing to give up? Be honest.

What are your human non-negotiables with Jesus? What are things or people you would say no to Jesus about?

Do you think right now you would be willing to walk away from what others think in order to follow what Jesus thinks?

What still scares you?

Verses for Meditation
Romans 13:11-12

Entering God's rest looks a lot different than religion makes it out to be. Most of us do not understand what His perfect peace and rest looks or feels like. Rest must be a serious issue with the church body since he is revealing it to us for a third time.

Matthew 11:28-30 "Come to me, all you who are weary and burdened, and I will give you rest. Take my yoke upon you and learn from me, for I am gentle and humble in heart, and you will find rest for your souls. For my yoke is easy and my burden is light."

As we talked about in Day 10, God himself took a rest day and made it Holy. What if we made our rest day holy? What if we could fully grasp what it means to come to Jesus with our burdens and give them fully to Him and just take on His yoke and His burden? Imagine if we stopped carrying our burdens. Truly take a minute to seek this understanding. This would totally change the way we live. It would make us shift our own hearts and minds to the plans of God vs our own agendas.

If I am not carrying around burdens that are mine from the world, how free would that feel?

Galatians 5:1 "It is for freedom that Christ has set us free. Stand firm, then, and do not let yourselves be burdened again by a yoke of slavery."

Challenge: Get in a quiet space and ask the Lord to reveal what burdens you are carrying. Now, fully submit them into the arms of Jesus! Crying out is okay in this moment because what follows is fully freedom to walk lightly into what He has planned!

What burdens are you carrying? How does it feel to you?

What do you think Jesus' burdens are? How do you think they feel vs yours?

How is your rest going to look now that you have no burdens of your own?

Verses for Meditation
2 Corinthians 3:16-18

STEP 5- SOAK IN IT

DAY 13- ADVENTURE AWAITS

When we look at the life and ministry of Jesus, it is full of adventure and excitement! He walked the life of adventure and did what his Father wanted, even when it did not make sense to the world. What if we walked so boldly and freely in everyday life like Jesus? When the Lord says in your heart to stop and speak to a stranger, do we obey? When He says give a particular amount to someone or a ministry when it does not seem logical financially, do we obey? What would the world look like if we obeyed the direct word of the Lord?

Psalm 143:10 "Teach me to do your will, for you are my God; may your good Spirit lead me on level ground."

When we can surrender our hearts and minds to understand that God is fully in control of each detail of our lives, we can start to understand how fun and adventurous it can be! When you get excited to sleep at night because you know the Lord is going to give you a dream or vision of the next step, that is a life of adventure. When you wake up, ask the Lord, "What do you desire for me to do today?" If he presses something uncomfortable on your heart, but you know the outcome will be amazing, you are entering a life of adventure.

An adventurous life is exciting and fun! You find joy in the unknown and mystery of God. How do we know the mysteries and find the adventure?

Jeremiah 33:3 "Call to me and I will answer you and tell you great and unsearchable things you do not know."

God LOVES revealing more and more to us when we seek Him and simply ask! There is a level of obedience and patience that is required to get further and further into deeper communication with Jesus. It may even require some fasting and praying so communication is clearer. He may even need to reveal some things that block you from communication with the Holy One. For example, sin(s) you haven't given to Him, attacks from the enemy that require prayer battle or even just our human nature making us doubt in the spiritual realm. Is it "human nature" or deception that makes us doubt the Spiritual realm? Accepting Spiritual, supernatural experiences may actually be what God planned as a component to our human nature.

Challenge: Continue to ask the Lord if there is anything blocking you from clear communication with Him. Write down any time that you felt really pressed to give something specific to someone or that the Lord wanted you to speak something. Thank Him for those moments of obedience or ask forgiveness for any disobedience when you justified not doing what He wanted you to do.

What do you feel God has opened your eyes to see that maybe others don't see (in scripture or an issue in the world)?

What path do you feel drawn to or that the Lord is pressing on you? (for example, ministering more to your family or a specific cause you feel passionate about)?

In your "perfect world," what would an adventurous life look like? Dream Big here!

Verses for Meditation
Mark 10: 35-45

2 Timothy 1:7 "For the Spirit God gave us does not make us timid, but gives us power, love and self-discipline."

The only fear we should possess is the fear of the Lord. Most people take this fear as a bad kind of fear but really it is something to delight in! It's kind of like riding a roller coaster, you are slowly moving up the massive hill and you feel the fear of the height and speed that is about to take place but it's more of an excitement kind of fear vs actual terror. Then when you crest the top of the hill and fly down and around, you may still have some fear of the moment, but it brings utter delight and laughter! That is how the fear of the Lord works! You trust the path and design of the roller coaster enough to place your life in the cart, and even though it can be scary during some parts, it's a fun ride and you want all your friends there with you!

Isaiah 11:3 "He will delight in the fear of the LORD. He will not judge by what he sees with his eyes or decide by what he hears with his ears."

Outside of the fear of the Lord, the one thing that will stop you from living in God's perfect will is the enemy's spirit of fear. Fear is what stops us from getting up and saying or doing what God has called us to do. What God wants us to do may not be popular in the world's eyes, even your family may reject the idea. You must decide what path you want to take. Will you allow the spirit of fear to control you or will you allow the fear of the Lord to direct your path?

Challenge: Look up as many verses about fear as you can. Find out what God says about the difference between fear of the Lord vs worldly fear.

Are you a slave to fear? What are you saying no to because you are afraid?

What does full surrender to the fear of the Lord look like in your life? (If you don't know, ask)

What can you do this week to boldly display that you are a fearless child of God?

Verses for Meditation
Isaiah 11: 1-5

What does "But seek first the kingdom of God" really mean? What does God's Kingdom mean for me on earth? When we pray the Lord's Prayer, what does, "as it is in heaven" look like on earth?

Most of us have prayed the Lord's Prayer repeatedly to the point of memorization.

Matthew 6: 9-10 "Our Father in heaven, hollowed be your name, your kingdom come, your will be done, on earth as it is in heaven."

How many of us are praying this but don't mean it? Are we living as though we truly believe that it can be on earth as it really is in heaven? When we live in a poverty mindset or think we will always have a 'chronic' sickness; are we really believing in the power of heaven? Does heaven not have streets of gold and sickness does not exist? Do we not believe in the power of the Holy Spirit to heal even what the human doctor says we must live with?

Matthew 6:33 "But seek first his kingdom and his righteousness, and all these things will be given to you as well."

If we seek first the kingdom of God in everything, how much struggle would we avoid trying to do it in our own power? Why do we try to do everything ourselves first, fail and then try picking up the pieces when we should just surrender our situation to God FIRST and leave all our troubles in His hands?

Psalm 9:9-10 "The Lord is a refuge for the oppressed, a stronghold in times of trouble. Those who know your name trust in you, for you, Lord, have never forsaken those who seek you."

Challenge: Write to the Lord listing all your current struggles, roadblocks, or even physical issues. Seek Him FIRST on all you listed and ask him with ALL Authority (that Jesus left with us through the Holy Spirit) to fix, move, and heal all of them in the Name of Jesus Christ! Do this with the backing and confidence of heaven!

What are you trying to do in your own power without the help of Jesus (maybe because you think it's just for you or too small of an issue for God)?

Do you think God wants you to cast all your cares (even the small ones) on Him?

Why do you doubt heaven? Why do you doubt the power and authority Jesus died to give you? What still scares you?

Verses for Meditation
Luke 11:11-13

DAY 16-- WHO DOES GOD SAY YOU ARE?

God created you in His likeness and image to be His children. How much do you love your children? Would you do anything for them?

> *Genesis 1: 27 "So God created mankind in his own image, in the image of God he created them; male and female he created them."*

God did not make a mistake when he formed you in your mother's womb. He created each one of us with purpose and to be heirs of His Kingdom! We just need to accept our worth and value in the Kingdom! How much are we helping or hurting the kingdom in how we live? Each life has such high value in God's eyes.

We are Prince and Princesses of the King of kings and Lord of lords! We have an eternal inheritance that no human or thing can destroy!

> *1 Peter 1:3-5 "Praise be to the God and Father of our Lord Jesus Christ! In his great mercy he has given us new birth into a living hope through the resurrection of Jesus Christ from the dead, and into an inheritance that can never perish, spoil or fade. This inheritance is kept in heaven for you, who through faith are shielded by God's power until the coming of the salvation that is ready to be revealed in the last time."*

What lies are you believing about your worth? What does God want you to believe?

> *John 10:10 "The thief comes only to steal and kill and destroy; I have come that they may have life and have it to the full."*

Challenge: What do you feel your life is worth? List what you would be willing to die for. Now, relate that to what God was and is willing to do for you, His child.

What are you saying to yourself in the mirror? What do you see and believe?

How important do you feel like you are in the world? Why? Be honest.

What can we change to help our Father's Kingdom (our inheritance) vs hurt it?

Verses for Meditation
1 Peter 1:13-16

Much of the body of Christ has not been operating in the gifts of the Holy Spirit for so long that God cannot use his Children to the fullest. Why do we get hurt at church? Why does the responsibility to operate in or out of the church walls fall on a few people that get burned out?

Jesus called everyone to operate like a body and the body is sick right now and not able to be what He has called us to be and operate the way He called us to operate. Jesus did not create all the thousands of denominations of churches we have created. He wanted us all working and drinking from the same Spirit!

1 Corinthians 12:12-13 "Just as a body, though one, has many parts, but all its many parts forms one body, so it is with Christ. For we were all baptized by one Spirit so as to form one body-- whether Jews or Gentiles, slave or free-- and we were all given the one Spirit to drink."

Once we allow the Spirit to flow freely, He then can give amazing gifts to his children so they can start operating fully in the Spirit. What are these gifts?

1 Corinthians 12:7-11 "Now to each one the manifestation of the Spirit is given for the common good. To one there is given through the Spirit a message of wisdom, to another a message of knowledge by means of the same Spirit, to another faith by the same Spirit, to another gifts of healing by that one Spirit, to another miraculous powers, to another prophecy, to another distinguishing between spirits, to another speaking in different kinds of tongues, and to still another the interpretation of tongues. All these are the work of one and the same Spirit, and he distributes them to each one, just as he determines."

Why do we depend on the "Pastor" of each church to carry the load of the body? What gifts and miraculous things could happen if we all got filled with the Holy Spirit and He started giving these gifts out to the body of Christ and we USED them?

Challenge: Ask the Lord to fill your body with the Holy Spirit and Surrender everything! Then ask what gifts he wants you to have! Be patient with the answer. Remember we are on God's time, not earthly time. He may need some consistent obedience and patience until he answers, but He knows the desires of your heart!

Do you feel the Holy Spirit in your body? If so, has he showed you any gifts listed in 1 Corinthians 12 that you have?

Are we making these gifts weird? Do you get freaked out if you hear the gift of tongues? Why?

If you desired the gifts, what would you desire? Talk with the Holy Spirit about the desires of your heart.

Verses for Meditation
1 Corinthians 12:14-31

Philippians 4:8 "Finally, brothers and sisters, whatever is true, whatever is noble, whatever is right, whatever is pure, whatever is lovely, whatever is admirable-- if anything is excellent or praiseworthy-- think about such things."

God wants us to fill our hearts and minds with so much good that we can easily discern the lie or any attack from the other side. If we think on such things that are true, noble, right, pure, lovely and admirable; imagine how each day would change for the good! We must do even our small task with excellence, even if it is cleaning our home or smiling at a stranger. Small things make up big differences.

We, also, need to put on our armor to make it through each day successfully! The world is a battle zone, and the enemy is there to get us off our perfect path even just slightly. If we are ready for the battle, then we can fight it easily and with great authority and backing of heaven!

Ephesians 6:10-12 "Finally, be strong in the Lord and in his mighty power. Put on the full armor of God, that you can take your stand against the devil's schemes. For our struggle is not against flesh and blood, but against the rulers, against the authorities, against the powers of this dark world and against the spiritual forces of evil in the heavenly realms."

Remember, we are not against people of the world but the darkness that is holding them in bondage or making them do things against God's will. God's creation is good, but we allow darkness to block our light.

Challenge: Think through your morning routine, daily task, and evening routines. What can we do with Philippians 4:8 in mind and how can we do it successfully with our armor of God on?

What can you do better in your home, work, or church life better? What have we been doing halfway vs fully for God?

Do we still have too much on our calendars that is keeping us from succeeding? If we can't do everything out of excellence, what do we need to give up for this journey?

Are you putting on your armor of God every day and what does that really mean?

Verses for Mediation
Ephesians 6:13-20

PART 7- SALE

DAY 19- EVERYTHING OUT OF LOVE

We can do everything God wants, but if we do not do it out of love, nothing happens. It will just be one big mess. We can use our spiritual gifts but if we do it for a show, platform or to make us look good vs out of REAL love from the Father, we are nothing!

1 Corinthians 13: 1-3 "If I speak in the tongues of men or of angels, but do not have love, I am only a resounding gong or a clanging cymbal. If I have the gift of prophecy and can fathom all mysteries and all knowledge, and if I have a faith that can move mountains, but do not have love, I am nothing. If I give all I possess to the poor and give over my body to hardship that I may boast, but do not have love, I gain nothing."

God needs us, as a body, to stop making church and gathering a show or performance. Performance is out of love of self and leaves no room for the Spirit to flow and the love of God to penetrate the heart. It is good to practice, learn and perfect our faith; but when it becomes about self, we sin.

Philippians 2:1-4 "Therefore if you have any encouragement from being united with Christ, if any comfort from his love, if any common sharing in the Spirit, if any tenderness and compassion, then make my joy complete by being likeminded, having the same love, being one in spirit and of one mind. Do nothing out of selfish ambition or vain conceit. Rather, in humility value others above yourselves, not looking to your own interest but each of you to the interest of others."

We can hurt people within our church walls if we become about self, and we don't operate in the same Spirit.

Challenge: Look at what you do right now within your church walls. Is everyone operating in the same Spirit out of love or is there tension somewhere? Ask for boldness in addressing this matter out of love.

What have you done this week to show love (to family, people you know and people you don't know)?

How does Christ love differently from our humankind love? Which one is shining brighter?

What situation are you facing right now where it is hard to show Christ's love? What would Jesus do to resolve it?

Verses for Meditation
John 3:16-21

God has given you everything you need right now to operate in His Spirit with love and truth. Do not say that you have nothing to give right now, because you have everything to lose. Do you want to gain eternal rewards or ones that can be destroyed here on earth?

Revelation 22:12 "Look, I am coming soon! My reward is with me, and I will give to each person according to what they have done. I am the Alpha and the Omega, the First and the Last, the Beginning and the End. Blessed are those who wash their robes, that they may have the right to the tree of life and may go through the gates into the city."

Where has God placed you right now? The time is near, we do not have time to waste! Not only is our life short but the times on earth are short. Do you want to take as many people with you as possible or do you want to see them left behind? What does Jesus want for his Bride?

Revelation 1: 7 "Look, he is coming with the clouds, and every eye will see him, even those who pierced him; and all peoples on earth will mourn because of him. So shall it be! Amen."

It is now serious, church, to go forth and make disciples and send disciples out! We should not see our church walls as a country club but as a place we equip the saints and send them out! We have focused our priorities on the number of attendees, tithes coming through the door and the comfort of the pews; not on our TRUE commission from Jesus.

Matthew 28:19-20 "Therefore go and make disciples of all nations, baptizing them in the name of the Father and of the Son and of the Holy Spirit, and teaching them to obey everything I have commanded you. And surely I am with you always, to the very end of the age."

Challenge: Evaluate how you do "church." Are you there to check and block off the weekly task list and feel good or are you there to get equipped for going out when He calls you?

QUESTIONS

How comfortable are you at church? Are you just attending to feel good that week or are you there to gain knowledge on how to go outside the walls to preach, teach and baptize?

Do you think preaching, teaching, and baptizing is only for Pastors and Sunday School Teachers? Now, look at what the Bible says.

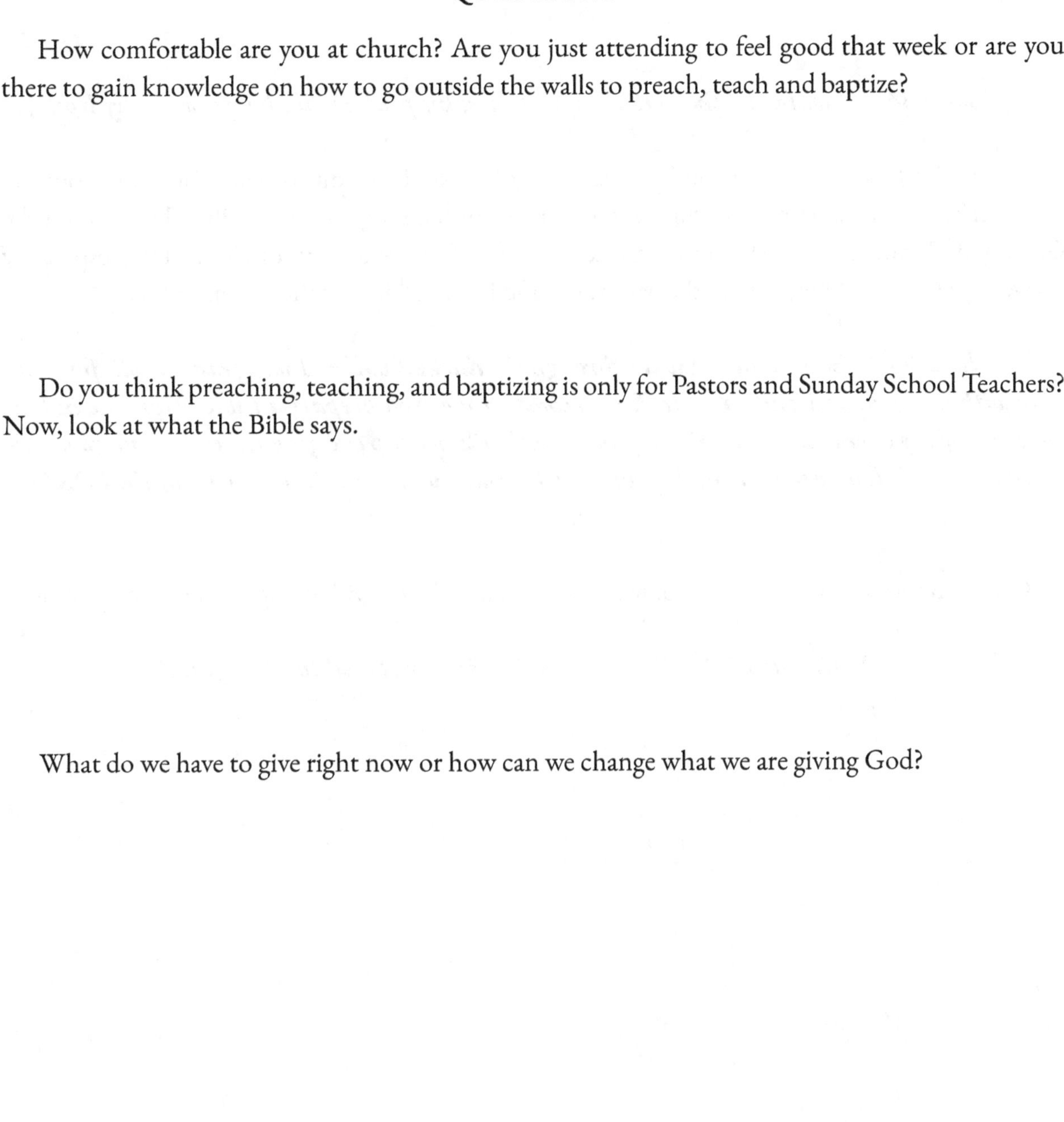

What do we have to give right now or how can we change what we are giving God?

Verses for Meditation
Jude 1:17-23

Psalm 34:1 "I will extol the LORD at all times; his praise will always be on my lips."

Let us give God all the glory and praise! We try to take the credit for what God does, but He is now raising His children up in this new movement of the Holy Spirit. It will only give Him the Glory and Honor and Praise! Do we want to be a part of the next move of God? How desperately do we long to praise Him, even in the hard times and in the middle of the storms of life?

Psalm 23:4-6 "Even though I walk through the darkest valley, I will fear no evil, for you are with me; your rod and your staff, they comfort me. You prepare a table before me in the presence of my enemies. You anoint my head with oil; my cup overflows. Surely your goodness and love will follow me all the days of my life, and I will dwell in the house of the LORD forever."

Can we honestly say that we do not fear death? Can we be ok with dying for the sake of Christ?

Philippians 1:21 "For to me, to live is Christ and to die is gain."

Challenge: Now that you have come to the completion of this 21-day journey of full surrender that has given you freedom; the REAL journey is just now starting! Write out a prayer to God the Father, Jesus the Son and the Holy Spirit giving all praise and gratitude for changing your life and giving you the inheritance of eternity with them! Keep this prayer for future generations to use as a testimony about them!

Do you know where you will spend eternity? If so, find scripture to comfort any fears you may have of death.

How do you praise God (song, words, your lifestyle)?

Now, how will you impact not only your close circle of family and friends, but others for Christ?

Verses for Meditation
Revelation 21:1-7